Usborne English Readers

Starter Level

The Fox and the Stork

Retold by Andy Prentice

Illustrated by Tania Rex

English language consultant: Peter Viney

Contents

≪≪≪

3

The Fox and the Stork

≪≪≪

16

Animal homes

≪≪≪

17

Activities

≪≪≪

22

Word list

You can listen to the story online here:
usborne.com/foxandstorkaudio

This is Fox with her friends.
Fox loves to play tricks.

My tricks are really funny.

Her friends don't laugh. Some tricks are not funny. Some tricks are not nice. Some tricks can hurt.

Fox, please stop it.

Fox doesn't listen to them. She just wants to play more and more tricks.

One day, Fox sees her friend Stork.
Stork is a bird. He stands in the water
and catches fish with his long beak.

Fox watches and waits. She has an
idea, an idea for a new trick.

"Hey, Stork! Come and have a meal at my house," Fox says. "I can cook for you. I can make you something really good."

Ooh, yes please.

Stork is happy. He is not catching many fish today. He is very hungry.

Fox quickly runs home. She cooks fish soup. Fox makes really good soup. She eats some. The soup is delicious.

Stork walks under the tall trees to Fox's house. He can smell the soup. He really wants to eat it.

"Please, sit down, my friend." says Fox. She puts a big bowl of fish soup in front of Stork.

The bowl is very flat. Stork tries to eat the soup with his long beak, but he can't.

What is this?

"Oh, this soup is really good,"
says Fox. "Don't you like it?"

"I can't eat it," says Stork. "My beak
is very long and my bowl is flat."

Can't you see?

Fox eats all her delicious soup.
Stork watches her sadly. He can't eat
anything, but he can smell it.

"Hahaha!" Fox laughs. "This is a
really funny trick!"

Stork doesn't laugh. He doesn't
say anything. He is still really hungry.
He is angry, but now he has an idea
for a trick, too.

The next morning, he meets Fox by the water again.

"Hey Fox! Come and have a meal at my house this evening," he says.

Ooh, yes please.

Fox walks under the tall trees.
Soon she can smell Stork's meal.

"Hello, Fox," says Stork. "Please, sit
down. I am making *my* fish soup today."
"Oh, good. I love fish soup," says Fox.

Stork puts a tall, thin jar of fish soup in front of Fox.

Fox tries to eat the soup, but she can't. She can just smell the delicious soup in the jar.

"Hey, Stork!" says Fox. "I'm really hungry. This isn't funny!"

Stork eats all his soup. Fox is angry.
"You can't do this to me," she says.
"I play tricks, not you!"

Stork smiles. "I know. You play
tricks on all the other animals and you
laugh. Tricks are funny, you say – but
are they really?"

Fox, you are
my friend.

I like you,
but you need
to learn.

"Oh…" says Fox. "I understand now. Tricks aren't always funny. I can stop my tricks."

"Very good," says Stork. "Well done, Fox."

He gives Fox a big bowl of soup. It is delicious.

Animal homes

Animals live in all kinds of homes.

Birds make nests for
their eggs and baby birds.

Storks make
very big nests.

Nest

Earth

Some animals, like
rabbits, badgers and foxes,
live under the ground.

A fox's underground
home is called
its earth.

Can you think of some more animals?
Do you know about their homes?

Activities
The answers are on page 24.

Can you see these things in the picture?
Which three things *can't* you see?

beak boat book bowl door flower
fox horse house soup stork tail

Which animal?

Choose Fox or Stork.

Which animal…

A. …loves to play tricks?

B. …has a long beak and catches fish?

C. …has an idea for a new trick?

D. …says "I play tricks, not you"?

E. …says "I like you, but you need to learn"?

F. …says "Very good" and "Well done"?

Where are they?

Look at the picture of Fox and her friends, then choose the right words for the sentences.

1. .... is up in the tree.
2. .... is behind Tortoise.
3. .... is on the ground.
4. .... is between Stork and ....
5. .... is between Badger and Owl.

Is that right?

Are these sentences true?

A. Fox's soup is delicious.
B. Stork isn't hungry.

C. Fox can't eat her soup.
D. Stork is sad.

Fox's new trick

Match the words to the pictures.

1.

2.

3.

4.

A.
This isn't funny.

B.
I have an idea for a new trick.

C.
I can stop my tricks.

D.
Don't you like my soup?

Word list

beak (n) birds have beaks. Their mouths and noses are in their beaks.

bowl (n) you eat food like soup or rice from bowls.

catch (v) to take hold of something that is moving. You catch animals, especially fish, for food.

cook (v) when you cook food, you make it ready or you make it hot so that it is good to eat.

delicious (adj) very good to eat.

flat (adj) when something is flat, it doesn't have high or deep parts. For example, plates are flat.

fox (n) a small red-brown animal. A fox is a kind of wild dog.

fox

flat bowl

idea (n) when you think of something new, you have an idea.

jar (n) you can put food, water or other liquids in jars. Jars are usually small or narrow.

play tricks (v) when you play tricks, you tell someone something that isn't true, or surprise them in an unkind way.

smell (v) you smell things, for example food or flowers, with your nose.

soup (n) a kind of food that you can make from meat, fish or vegetables.

stork (n) a big bird with very long legs.

tall (n) tall things are high or a long way from the gound. People, animals, trees and houses can all be tall.

thin (adj) the opposite of thick or fat.

beak

tall,
thin jar

stork

Answers

Can you see these things in the picture?

Three things you can't see: boat, book, horse.

Which animal?

Fox: A, C, D
Stork: B, E, F

Where are they?

1. Owl
2. Fox
3. Tortoise
4. Badger, Rabbit
5. Stork

Is that right?

Sentences A and D are true.

Fox's new trick

1. B
2. D
3. A
4. C

You can find information about other Usborne English Readers here: usborne.com/englishreaders

Designed by Hope Reynolds
Series designer: Laura Nelson Norris
Edited by Mairi Mackinnon

First published in 2022 by Usborne Publishing Ltd., Usborne House, 83-85 Saffron Hill, London EC1N 8RT, England. usborne.com Copyright © 2022 Usborne Publishing Ltd.